Hello, Duck!

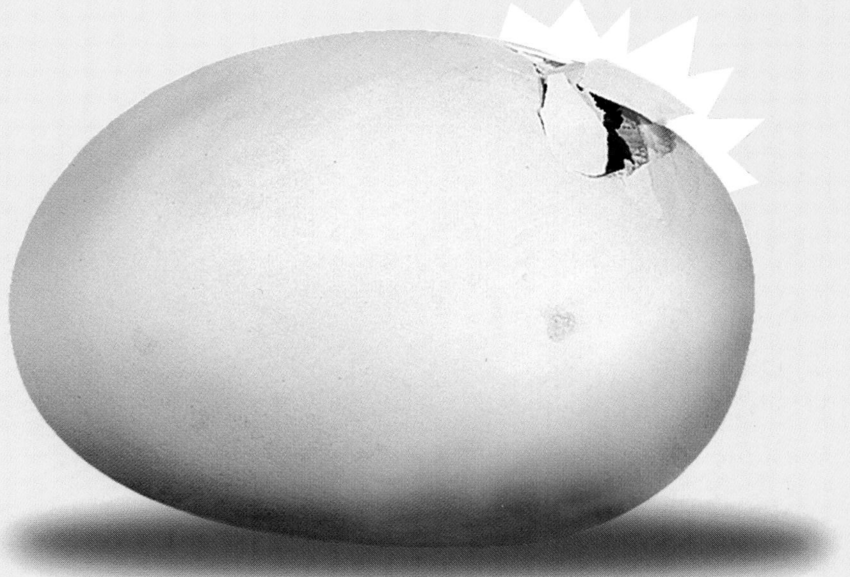

by Lada Kratky

HAMPTON-BROWN

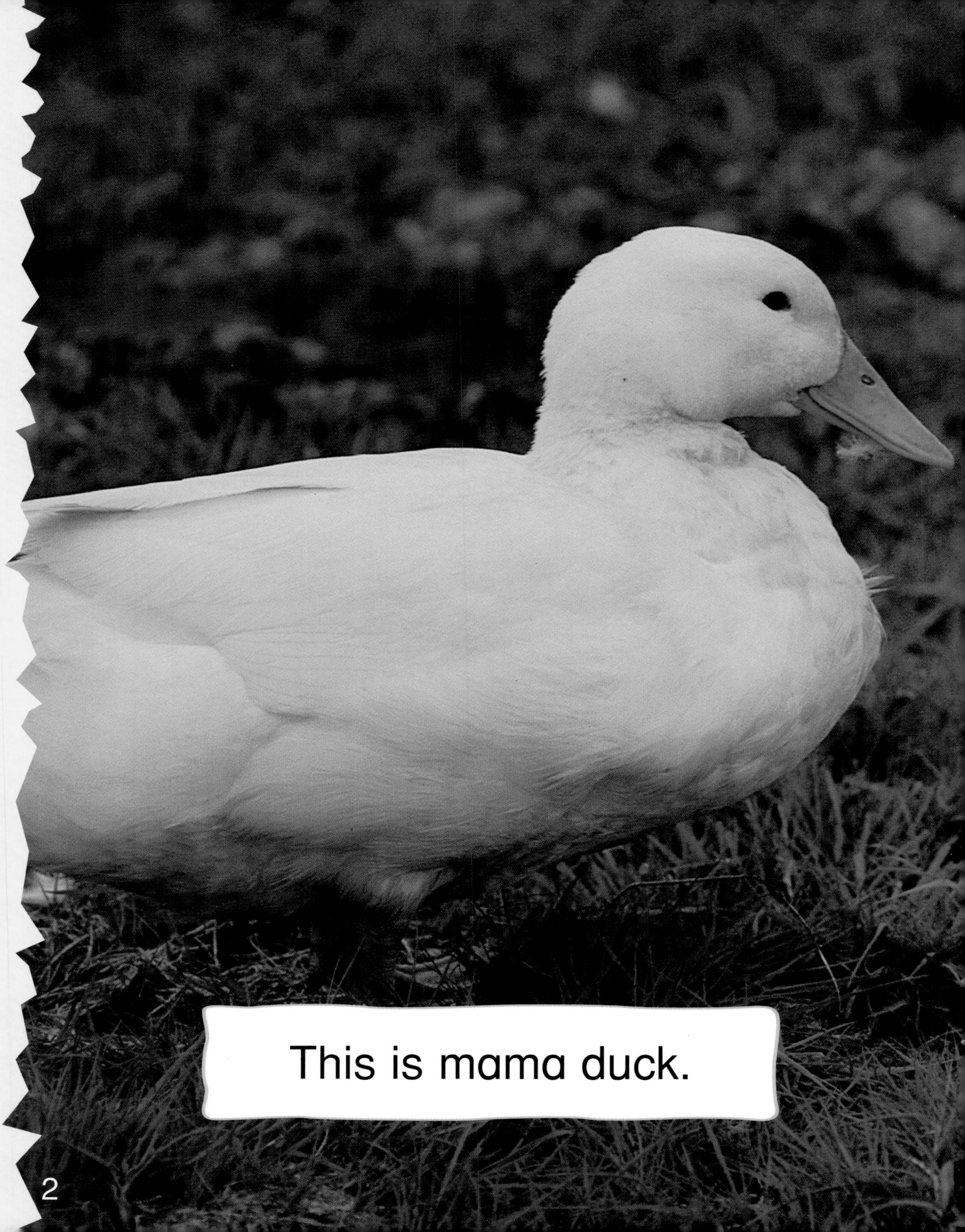

This is mama duck.

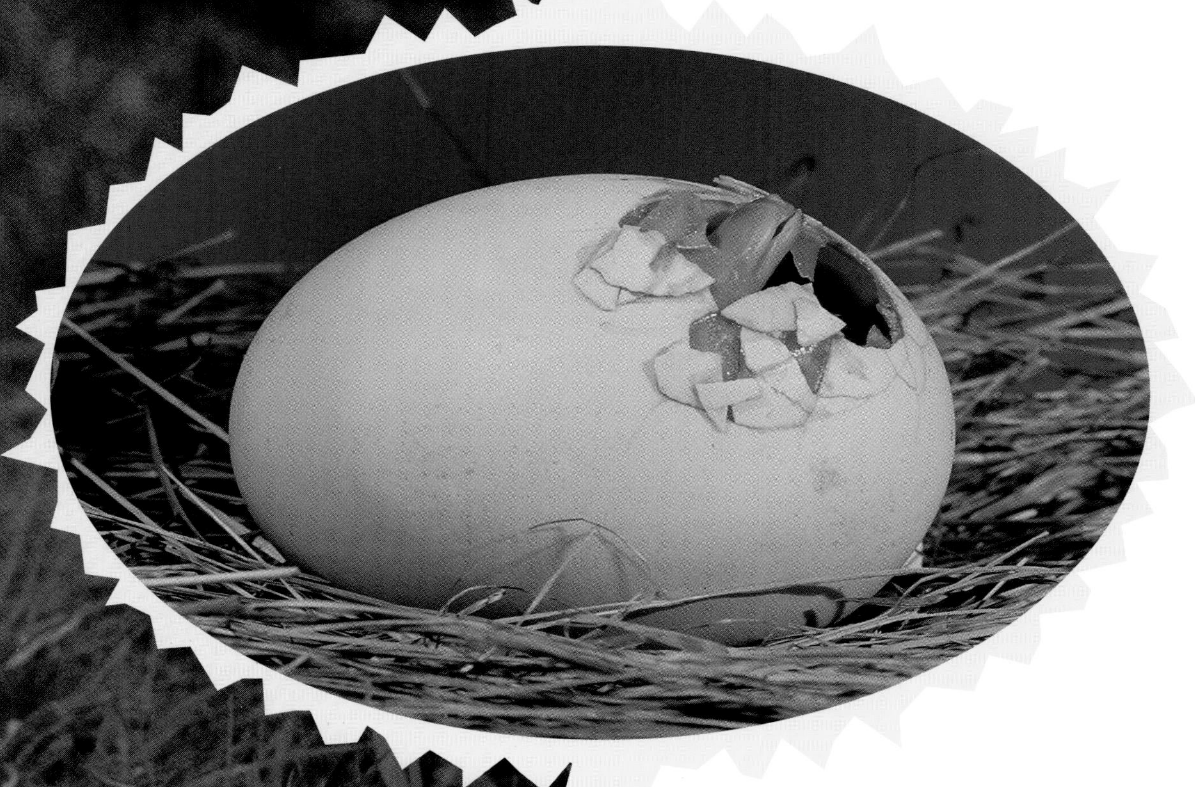

This is one of her eggs.

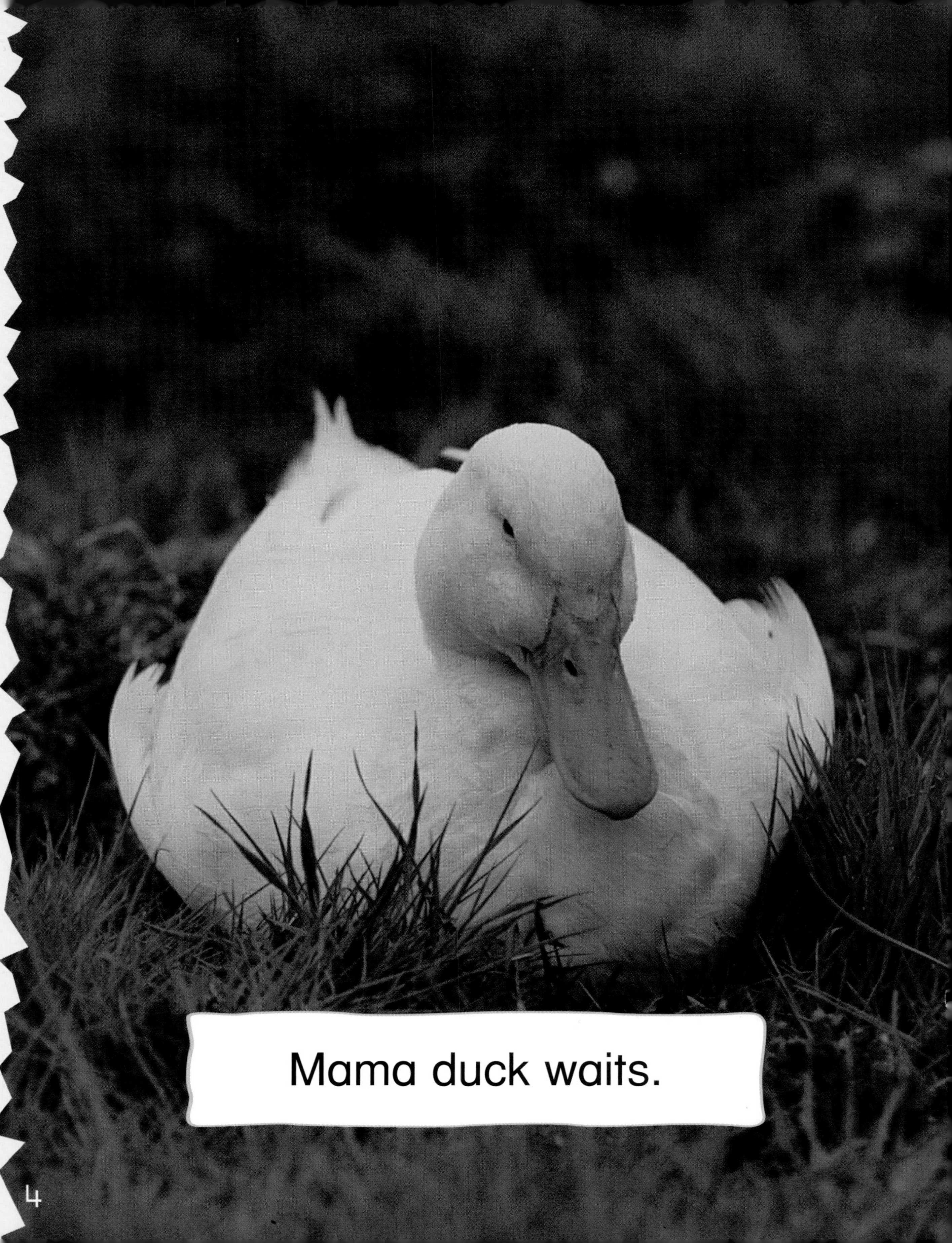

Mama duck waits.

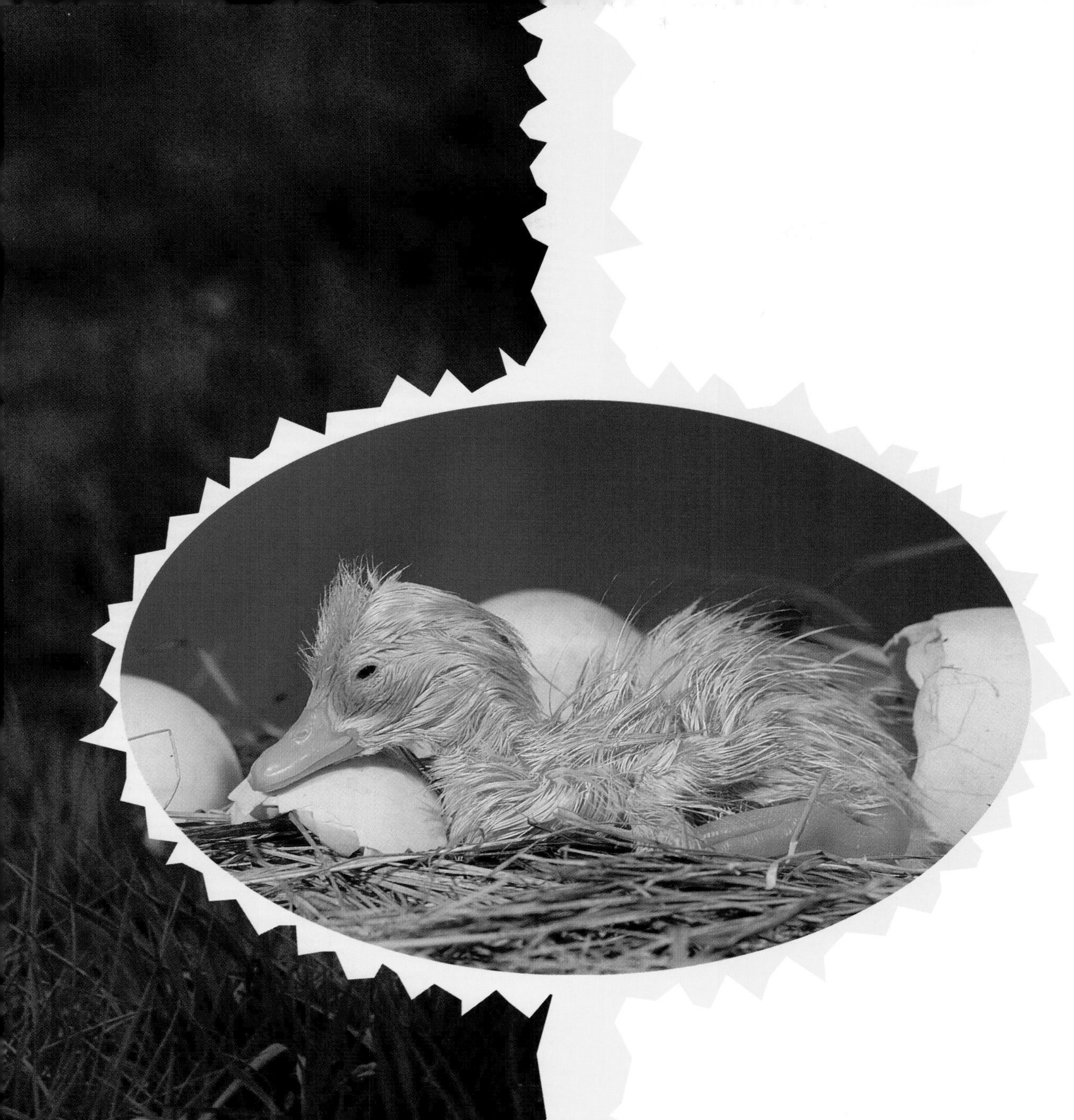

A baby duck hatches.

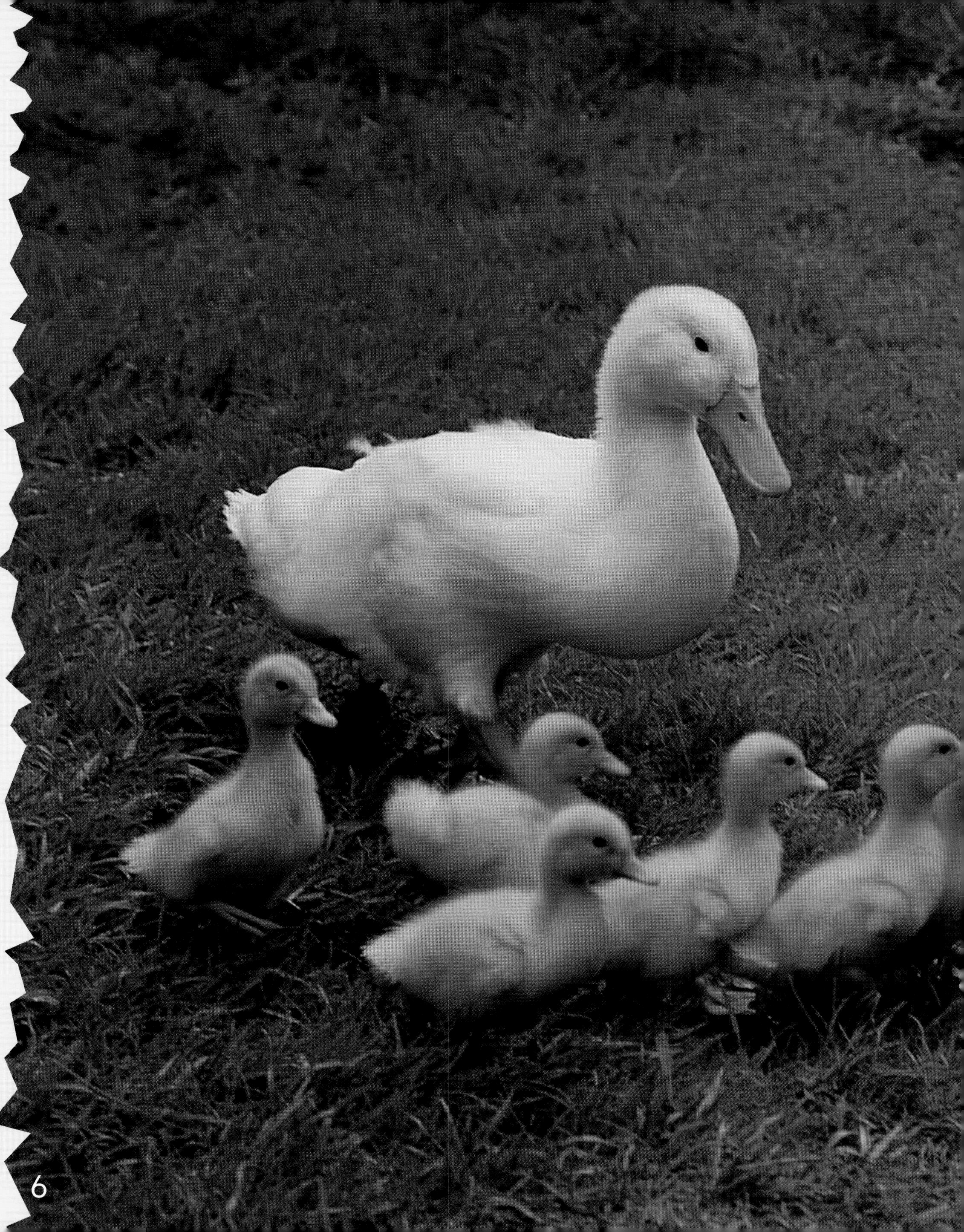

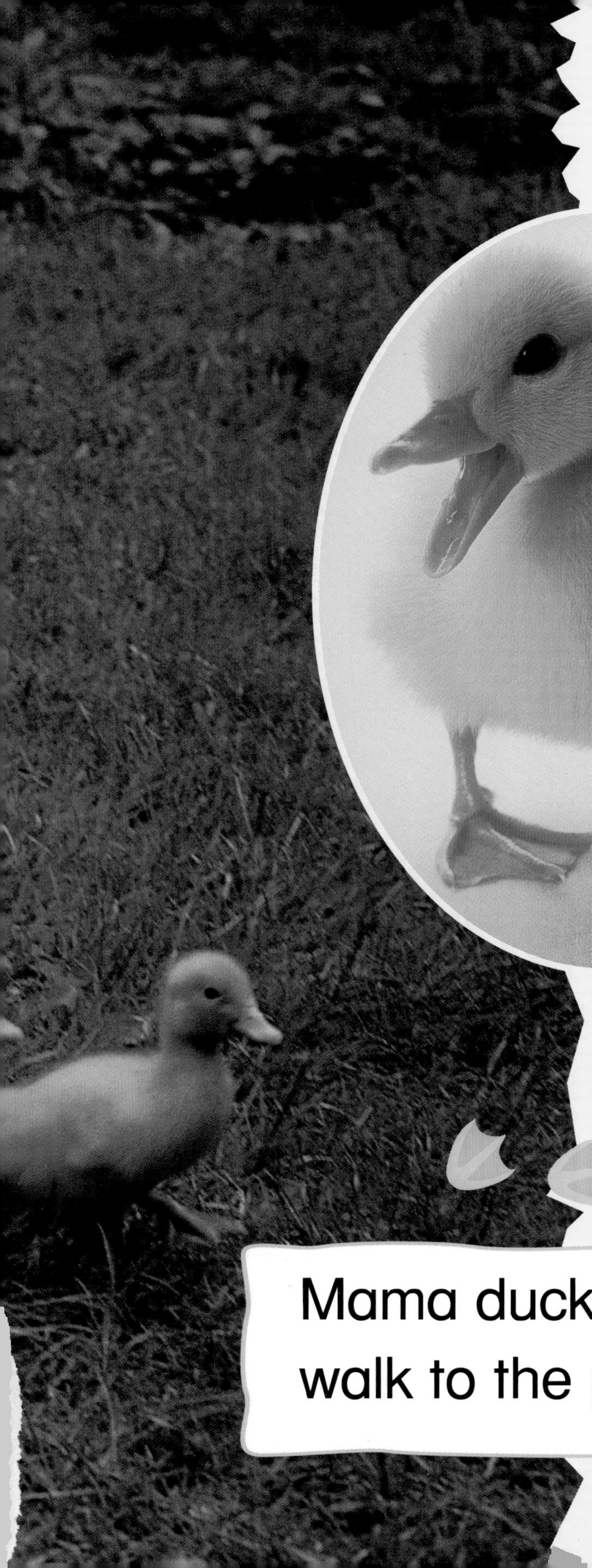

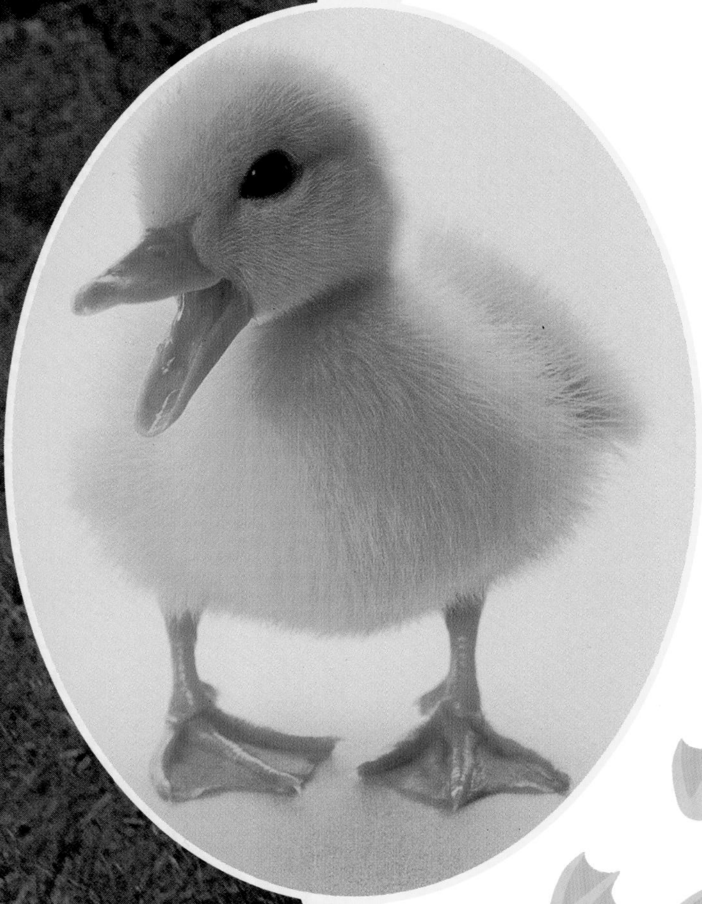

Mama duck and her babies walk to the pond.

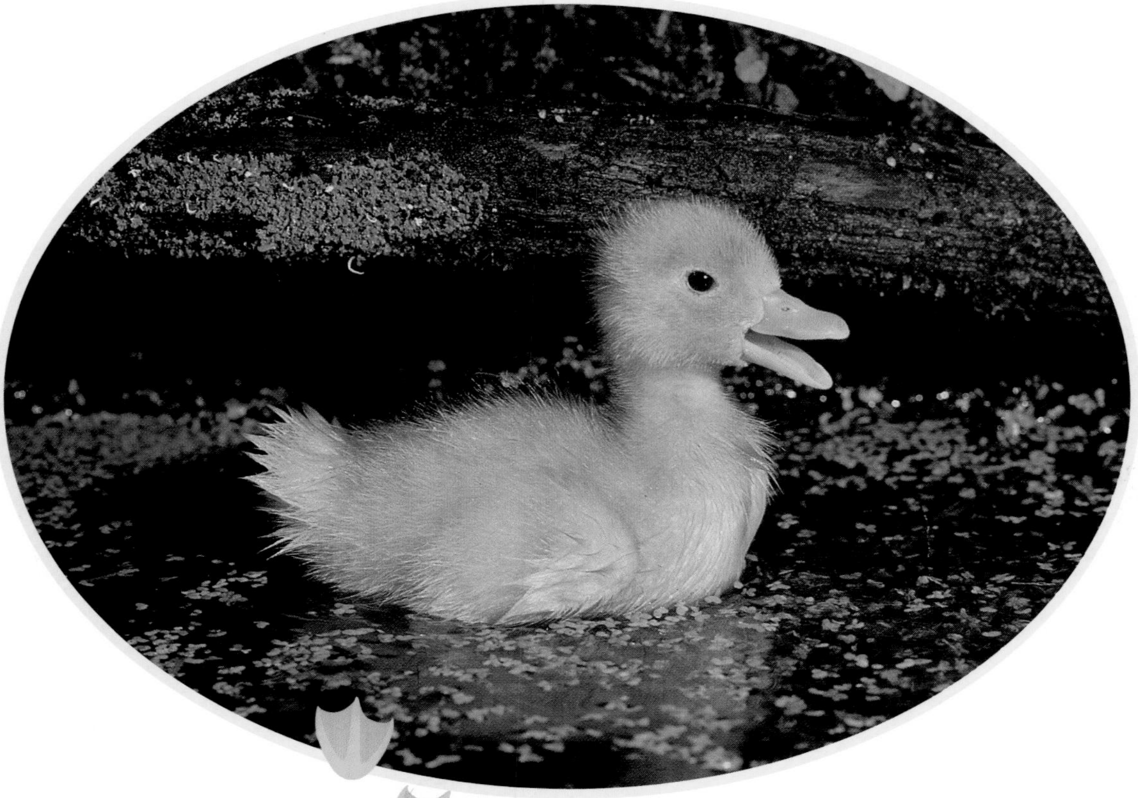

They go for a swim!